1 Introducing Tom Hanks

Today Tom Hanks can afford
to turn down $20 million.
He was offered this to make a film
but he doesn't want the stress.

He is the Hollywood actor
who can do no wrong.
Whatever he does, the world loves him.
He is Mr Nice Guy.
He is one of the most popular actors
in Hollywood.

There were no clues in his childhood
to show the star he was going to be.

2 Childhood

Tom was born
on 9 July 1956 in California.
He was the third of four children.

When Tom was five years old
his parents split up.
They never spoke to each other again.
Tom's baby brother Jim
stayed with his Mum.
She married again
another three times.

Tom, Larry and Sandra
stayed with their dad.
He re-married twice.
Tom's dad was a chef.
They moved house many times
as he moved jobs.

Tom was the third of four children.

Tom was a shy boy
but moving school so many times
helped him to cope with it.
He says
'In the end I had
three mothers, four fathers, five schools,
ten houses, three brothers and sisters
and eight step-brothers and sisters.'

Tom says his childhood was wonderful
and it made him strong.

3 Early Days in Drama

In High School Tom joined the drama club
because it looked like fun.
He was always the class clown
to mask his shyness.
Even so,
in 1974 he won his first Best Actor award
for his part in a school play.

After leaving school Tom went to college.
He joined a drama class there
to pass the time.
He was soon hooked
on everything to do with acting.

So Tom left college
and joined a drama course
at California University.

At first Tom wanted to be
a stage carpenter.
But he also acted and he was good.
He was happy on stage.

Before the end of his University course,
Tom was given paid work.
He could not resist.
He dropped out of University
and went to work for a theatre festival in Ohio.
He was paid $50 a week.

Tom's girlfriend from University
came to join him in Ohio.
Her name was Samantha.

They seemed to be
on top of the world.

4 New York

Now Tom felt he was a real actor.
He wanted to go to New York
to get into the big time.

In 1978 Tom and Samantha
moved to New York.
They knew it would be hard
but they didn't know how hard.
There was no work for Tom
and Samantha was pregnant.

He said, 'We had a year and a half
of horrible, scary days.'

Their son Colin was born.
Two months later
Tom and Samantha got married.
Four years later
they adopted a baby girl.
They called her Elizabeth.

5 TV Work

After small parts in two films
and a lot of volunteer work,
Tom landed a star part in a TV sitcom.

It was about two friends
who have to dress in drag
to get rooms in a Women Only hotel.

Tom was called **Buffy** in the sitcom.
The show was called *Bosom Buddies*.
It was a big hit when it came out in 1980.

Tom was paid $9,000 a show.
It was more money
than he'd ever had before.

When the show ended
Tom went on to have parts
in *Taxi* and *Happy Days*.

As Buffy in *Bosom Buddies*.

6 Film Success

Tom made friends
with one of the stars of *Happy Days*.
His name was Ron Howard.

By 1983 Ron was a film director.
He gave Tom his big break in films.
He asked Tom to star in his film, *Splash*.
The film was about a man
who falls in love with a mermaid.

To everyone's surprise
Splash was a big hit.
Everyone in it went on to be a star.

In the film *Splash* with Daryl Hannah. © Disney Enterprises, Inc.

7 Bad Films

For the next few years
Tom said yes to every film
he was asked to do.
He made some pretty bad films.
But he worked non-stop.
He was often away from home.
His marriage broke up in 1985.

In 1985 Tom was in Mexico
making a film called *Volunteers*.
The film was not a success at the box office.

But it was a success for Tom.
He fell in love with his co-star.
Her name was Rita Wilson.

Tom asked Rita to marry him
on New Year's Eve in 1987.
They were married on 30 April 1988.
Today they are still one of
Hollywood's happiest couples.

Tom and Rita married in 1988.

8 *BIG* Success

1988 was also a good year
for Tom's career.
He made his first blockbuster film.
It was called *Big*.

It's the story of a twelve year old boy
who wants to be big.
He gets his wish.

Tom plays the boy in a man's body.
He was nominated for an Oscar
for this film.

In the next three years
Tom made four more films
with no success.

The best thing in those years
was the birth of Tom and Rita's first son.
He was born in 1990
and they called him Chet.
This time Tom had time
to be a better dad.
He spent a lot of time with Chet.

9 A Romantic Part

By 1993 Tom was back
at the top of Hollywood's list of best actors.
But this time it wasn't a comedy.
It was a romantic film.

Sleepless in Seattle
was the story of a man
bringing up his ten year old son
on his own.

Tom's co-star was Meg Ryan
but Rita also had a part in the film.
Sleepless in Seattle
made everyone cry.
It was a big box-office success.
Tom proved he could play romantic parts.

With Meg Ryan in the film *Sleepless in Seattle.*

10 Taking Risks

In the same year
Tom took a big risk with his next job.
He starred in the film *Philadelphia*.

It's the story of a young lawyer.
He gets the sack
when his law firm finds out he has AIDS.
He goes on to sue his law firm.

Hollywood was not sure
that the public would like this film.
People said that
Tom couldn't play a gay man.

But they were wrong.

Tom won his first Oscar
for *Philadelphia*.
It was twenty years
after his first Best Actor award.
But it was worth waiting for.

When he got the Oscar
Tom thanked his teachers
from his school days.

Tom also took a risk
with his next film in 1994.
It was part comedy, love story
and history lesson.
It tells the story of a simple man
who becomes an American hero.

It was called *Forrest Gump*.
The public loved it.

Tom won an Oscar for *Forrest Gump*.

'Gump mania' swept the world.
Lines from the film became famous
like, 'Life is like a box of chocolates …'.

Tom won an Oscar
for the second year running.
He took a low wage
and a slice of the profits from the film.
It was a risk
but he ended up with $40 million.

Forrest Gump was still at the top in 1995.
Tom started to make his next film.
It was directed by Ron Howard.
It was called *Apollo 13*.

11 Being an Astronaut!

Tom played the astronaut Jim Lovell.
It is the true story
of the 1970 space flight
that went wrong.

They were going to land on the moon
but an oxygen tank blew up.
The astronauts were in great danger.
They were 205,000 miles from home.

They just made it back home
and Jim Lovell became a hero.

Apollo 13 was a dream come true for Tom.
He said, 'Every little boy
wants to play an astronaut'.

They filmed for ten days in a jet plane.
The plane kept flying up and over
with power dives.
This let them film in zero gravity
but it made everyone sick.
They called the plane
The Vomit Comet.

After *Apollo 13*
Tom said he was going to relax.
He spent time sailing, swimming
and playing golf.

In December 1995
Rita and Tom's second son was born.
They called him Truman.
Tom spent the whole of 1996
looking after Truman.

Tom attending the Venice Film Festival in September 1994.

12 More Films

After his long rest,
Tom made *Saving Private Ryan* in 1998.
It was a World War II story.
It was filmed in England and Ireland.
In the film,
Tom takes his men behind enemy lines
to find Private Ryan.

Tom had a great time making the film.
He said, 'It was a joy'.
He only had one set of clothes.
It didn't matter if he got dirty.

Tom's next film in 1998
was *You've Got Mail*.
Again it was a romantic comedy
with Meg Ryan.

You've Got Mail
was very different from his last film.
Tom said,
'People say making romantic comedy
looks easy.
You've got to be joking'.

It took two hours each day
to have his make-up put on.
All the filming was done indoors.
It wasn't much fun to make.

Tom chose three
very different films next.
The Green Mile is set in prison
on Death Row.
The green mile is the carpet between
the cells and the electric chair.
Tom plays the head prison guard.
The film tells the story
of the prisoners on Death Row.

The Castaway
is the story of a man
who spends four years alone on a desert island.

Dino is the life story
of the actor and singer, **Dean Martin**.

Today Tom has the security
he didn't have as a child.
He lives in a $2 million house
with his family
next to the Pacific.

He is the Hollywood actor
who can do no wrong.